RAISE YOUR HAND

ORGANIZE AND VOLUNTEER

Christy Mihaly

DONATIONS

 Rourke™

Before Reading: *Building Background Knowledge and Vocabulary*

Building background knowledge can help children process new information and build upon what they already know. Before reading a book, it is important to tap into what children already know about the topic. This will help them develop their vocabulary and increase their reading comprehension.

Questions and Activities to Build Background Knowledge:

1. Look at the front cover of the book and read the title. What do you think this book will be about?
2. What do you already know about this topic?
3. Take a book walk and skim the pages. Look at the table of contents, photographs, captions, and bold words. Did these text features give you any information or predictions about what you will read in this book?

Vocabulary: *Vocabulary Is Key to Reading Comprehension*

Use the following directions to prompt a conversation about each word.

- Read the vocabulary words.
- What comes to mind when you see each word?
- What do you think each word means?

> **Vocabulary Words:**
> - activist
> - environment
> - fundraiser
> - gender-neutral
> - organize
> - volunteer

During Reading: *Reading for Meaning and Understanding*

To achieve deep comprehension of a book, children are encouraged to use close reading strategies. During reading, it is important to have children stop and make connections. These connections result in deeper analysis and understanding of a book.

 Close Reading a Text

During reading, have children stop and talk about the following:

- Any confusing parts
- Any unknown words
- Text to text, text to self, text to world connections
- The main idea in each chapter or heading

Encourage children to use context clues to determine the meaning of any unknown words. These strategies will help children learn to analyze the text more thoroughly as they read.

When you are finished reading this book, turn to the next-to-last page for **After Reading Questions** and an **Activity**.

TABLE OF CONTENTS

CAN YOU HELP?

Everyone needs help sometimes. A friend might not have enough to eat. Someone else faces bullying. You might need help if you're sick or in an accident.

Some issues affect an entire community. Are there people in your town who don't have warm clothes? Is your street littered with garbage?

You may worry about faraway problems, too. Disasters around the world send people fleeing from their homes.

Can you help? Yes, you can be an **activist**.

activist (AK-tuh-vist): a person who helps make positive change in an issue important to them

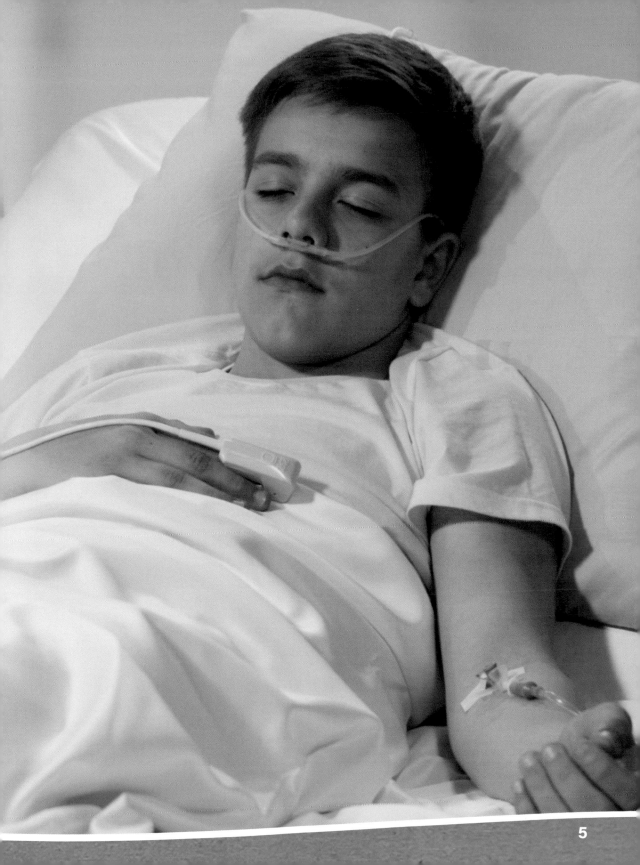

When Thomas Koska's teammates learned he had cancer, they stepped up. Thomas worried the treatments would make his hair fall out, so the members of the cross-country team and their coach shaved their heads.

Then his friends organized a mass head-shaving. Students and teachers lined up to get shaved in support of Thomas. As the razors buzzed, a crowd of supporters cheered them on.

Students also set up an online sign-up system for friends to make and deliver meals to help Thomas's family during his treatments.

You may not be able to fix everyone's problems yourself. But you can **volunteer** to help. And you can **organize**, getting others to join your efforts.

organize (OR-guh-nize): to bring people together in a joint action

volunteer (vah-luhn-TEER): to offer to help or do work without pay

WHAT CAN YOU DO?

VOLUNTEER—BE HAPPY!

Studies show that people who volunteer are happier people. Volunteering helps you meet interesting new people and learn new skills. Plus, it just feels good to help others and make a difference in the world.

How do you know where to start? Consider what you care about and what you're good at. Those things will guide you in picking a good way to help.

Maybe you've heard that a neighbor needs help because they lost their job, got sick, or had a new baby. If you're a cook, you can prepare and deliver food. Can't cook? Organize a schedule to let other people sign up to provide meals.

Or organize a **fundraiser**. Plan a neighborhood event to bring people together and raise money for baby supplies, food deliveries, or whatever your neighbor needs. You could also collect money online. There are lots of ways to help.

fundraiser (FUHND-ray-zur): an event held to collect money for a cause

Maybe you'd like to see more kindness at your school. If a new student joins the class, you could volunteer to be their friend. Ask the new kid to sit with you at lunch. Share a seat with them on the bus.

Think of creative ways you could show kindness to the whole school. For example, a group of students can stand at school entrances and greet people coming in with a *morning high five*. A sports team can organize morning high fives at a local elementary school.

Or start a *kindness rocks* project. Collect small stones, clean them, and paint them with colorful designs and cheerful messages. Then hide the stones around your school or neighborhood to spread the message of caring.

Look around your school. What changes would you like to see? Do you want a different dress code? **Gender-neutral** bathrooms? Do you have ideas to make students feel safer?

gender-neutral (JEN-dur NOO-truhl): suitable for all people, whether male, female, or any other identity

You can organize for change. Research the issues and brainstorm solutions. Identify people who can help. Spread the word and gather supporters.

Will your ideas cost money? Hold a fundraiser. What if your first attempt fails? Remember, change takes time.

There are many ways to raise your hand. Two Kentucky teens, Amelie Beck and Jacqueline Teague, were helping their older relatives sign up for COVID-19 vaccinations. They realized many older adults didn't understand the technology for registering online.

— THE DIANA AWARD —

England's Princess Diana believed that young people could change the world. In her honor, The Diana Award is given to young community activists around the world.

They wanted to do more. So, they started *VaxConnectKY* to walk people through the registration process. Their effort helped connect thousands of people with vaccines.

Sahana Vij wanted to fight hunger. She and her mom cooked homemade food for people at a local shelter. Then Sahana published a cookbook and said she'd donate the money from selling it to a group working to end hunger.

Katie Stagliano had a different idea. As a sixth-grader, she started Katie's Krops Garden-to-Table Dinners to serve fresh meals to hungry people. Her organization helps kids plant gardens and grow crops. The idea started when Katie brought a small cabbage plant home from a school project. She planted and watered it, and ended up growing a giant 40-pound cabbage. She gave the cabbage to a soup kitchen. It was so big, it helped feed 275 people. Katie decided to help other kids grow food. Katie's Krops has helped kids ages 9 to 16 grow more than 250,000 pounds of fruit and vegetables and provide food for many thousands of people.

If you want to help the **environment**, what can you do? New Jersey middle school student Sri Nihal Tammana wanted people to stop throwing old batteries into the trash. In landfills, batteries can leak and cause pollution.

Nihal organized to get batteries out of the trash. He set up bins where people could drop off dead batteries. He created a website explaining how to recycle batteries. He helped get thousands of batteries recycled.

environment: (en-VYE-ruhn-muhnt): nature and our surroundings on Earth

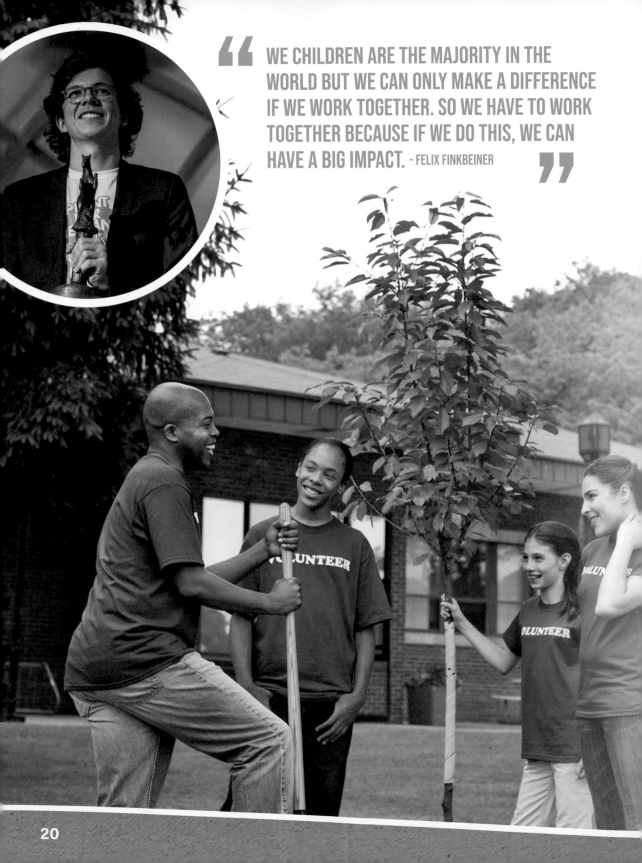

"WE CHILDREN ARE THE MAJORITY IN THE WORLD BUT WE CAN ONLY MAKE A DIFFERENCE IF WE WORK TOGETHER. SO WE HAVE TO WORK TOGETHER BECAUSE IF WE DO THIS, WE CAN HAVE A BIG IMPACT. - FELIX FINKBEINER"

Some problems may seem too big to solve. For example, climate change is a global issue. Don't let that stop you from getting involved.

Felix Finkbeiner learned how trees are critical to cooling the planet when he wrote a school report. He wrote about Wangari Maathai. She was an activist from Kenya who planted more than 30 million trees. Felix wondered what would happen if he organized kids to plant trees.

Felix started Plant-for-the-Planet, an organization that has helped young people plant millions of trees. At age 13, Felix spoke at the United Nations in New York. He told world leaders they should "stop talking and start planting."

FIND YOUR POWER

Some people prefer to work alone. That's okay. There are many ways one person can get involved.

One person can hold a sign or organize an online fundraiser. One person can write to government officials, demanding change. One person can make a difference.

You can also be an activist within your family. If you have learned about an issue that concerns you, share it with your family. For example, if you want less plastic in the ocean, look at your family's purchases. Can you substitute plastic-free products and reduce your home's plastic waste?

Sisters Melati and Isabel Wijsen grew up on the island of Bali, in Indonesia. The ocean near their home was full of plastic trash. When they went swimming, plastic bags wrapped around their arms. Together, they decided to do something about it.

In 2013, when they were 10 and 12, the Wijsen sisters started an organization called Bye Bye Plastic Bags. They called on the Bali government to ban single-use plastic bags. They gathered thousands of signatures on a petition and organized an enormous beach cleanup.

Their organization educated people about the plastic problem. Bali finally banned plastic bags in 2019. Then Melati and Isabel expanded their organization to help young activists get plastics banned in communities around the world.

SUMMER COMING

Wir sägen am dem Ast, auf dem wir alle sitzen!

SKOLSTREJK FÖR KLIMATET

Once you raise your hand, others may follow. Just ask Greta Thunberg. At age 15, she stood by herself at the Swedish Parliament holding a "School Strike for Climate Change" sign. She brought worldwide attention to the climate crisis and sparked actions around the globe.

So ... if you want to change something, stand up and get started!

SAVE THE PLANET

MEMORY GAME

Look at the pictures. What do you remember reading on the pages where each image appeared?

INDEX

AFTER-READING QUESTIONS

1. Think of something you'd like to change in your school or community. What's one thing you could do to make that change happen?
2. Do you believe that people who volunteer are happier than others? Why or why not?
3. Suppose you need to raise one thousand dollars for a cause that you care about. How would you begin?
4. What are some similarities between Katie Stagliano (who started Katie's Krops) and the Wijsen sisters (who started Bye Bye Plastic Bags)? In what ways are they, or their projects, different?
5. As an activist, would you prefer to work alone, with others, or both? Explain.

ACTIVITY

Get together with a friend or two and write a letter or email to ask for action on an issue that you care about. Explain the situation and how you think it could be improved. You could address the letter to a parent, teacher, principal, school board, or government or corporate official.

ABOUT THE AUTHOR

Author Christy Mihaly agrees with Princess Diana that young people have the power to change the world. She hopes readers of this book will use their power well. Christy also believes that books make the world better. A former lawyer, she has published more than thirty books for young readers.

www.rourkebooks.com

Quote Source: Hurst, Whitney. "The 13-year-old tree ambassador," CNN, February 23, 2011, http://www.cnn.com/2011/LIVING/02/23/teenage.tree.ambassador/index.html.

PHOTO CREDITS: page 1: © Halfpoint/ Getty Images; page 5: ©EvgeniyShkolenko/Getty Images; page 6–7: ©Brad Curtis; page 8: ©SDI Productions/ Getty Images, ©fstop123/Getty Images; page 10: ©SDI Productions/Getty Images; page 12: ©Thomas Faull / Getty Images; page 12–13: ©Julia Rendleman/Education Week; page 14–15: ©Christian Beck; page 15: ©Kent gavin Mirrorpix/Newscom; page 16: ©Ellen M. banner/The Seattle Times; page 17: ©Stacy Stagliano/Katie's Krops; page 19: ©artoleshko/Getty Images; page 20: ©Lino Mirgeler/dpa/picture-alliance/Newscom, ©Jupiterimages/ Getty Images; page 22–23: ©fizkes/Getty Images; page 24–25: ©apomares/ Getty Images; page 26–27:© twinsterphoto/ Getty Images, page 28–29: © Chris Emil JanßEn/ZUMA Press/Newscom

Edited by: Laura Malay
Cover and interior design by: Nick Pearson

Library of Congress PCN Data

Organize and Volunteer / Christy Mihaly
(Raise Your Hand)
ISBN 978-1-73165-288-1 (hard cover)(alk. paper)
ISBN 978-1-73165-258-4 (soft cover)
ISBN 978-1-73165-318-5 (e-book)
ISBN 978-1-73165-348-2 (e-pub)
Library of Congress Control Number: 2021952195

Rourke Educational Media
Printed in the United States of America
01-2412211937